# inspirations

# CUSHIONS

Over 20 beautiful projects for the home

**ínspirations**

# CUSHIONS

### Over 20 beautiful projects for the home

## ISABEL STANLEY

### PHOTOGRAPHY BY MARK WOOD

### AND ADRIAN TAYLOR

## LORENZ BOOKS

#### LONDON • NEW YORK • SYDNEY • BATH

This edition published in 1997 by Lorenz Books

Lorenz Books is an imprint of
Anness Publishing Limited
Hermes House
88–89 Blackfriars Road
London SE1 8HA

This edition is published in Canada by Lorenz Books, distributed
by Raincoast Books Distribution Limited, Vancouver.

© Anness Publishing Limited

ISBN 1 85967 430 5

A CIP catalogue record for this book is available from the British Library.

Publisher: Joanna Lorenz
Senior Editor: Clare Nicholson
Designer: Bobbie Colgate Stone
Stylists: Fanny Ward, Deena Beverly and Jenny Norton
Photography: Adrian Taylor and Mark Wood
Step-by-step Photography: Lucy Tizard

Printed and bound in Hong Kong

1 3 5 7 9 10 8 6 4 2

MEASUREMENTS
Both imperial and metric measurements have been given in the text. Where conversions produce an
awkward number, these have been rounded for convenience, but will produce an accurate result if one
system is used throughout.

# CONTENTS

# INTRODUCTION

THERE IS something luxurious, even indulgent, about cushions, because they only exist to make life more comfortable. They have a place in every room and, as long as they are not used too often for pillow fights, they will last for years and become old favourites with you and your family.

Besides the comfort that they provide, cushions can help you instantly transform your home by adding decorative detail to any interior. Use them to make dramatic changes to the feel of a sofa or the colour scheme of a room, simply by adding bright primary hues or soft neutral ones. Cushions can soften the hard seat of a dining-room chair or serve as the perfect stylish gift for a friend. Tuck a bolster behind your head as you curl up to read a book, or throw a pillow in the back of the car to serve as an outdoor seat when you go on a picnic.

*Inspirations: Cushions* clearly demonstrates, using step-by-step photography, how to make a wide selection of soft furnishings. There are sections covering the materials, equipment and basic techniques that you may need to attempt the projects featured. Take your inspiration from the designs, which range from basic cushions made from tea-towels to elaborate *objets d'art* embroidered with initials.

Don't restrict your endeavours to the standard square: cushions can be small, large, round or a bolster. Fabrics can be kept simple, or, alternatively, you could use a piece of antique tapestry or expensive brocade that you have coveted for a long time. Mix colours and patterns, add surface details, and create your own individual selection.

*Deborah Barker*

# EMBROIDERED HEART

*Warm wool blanketing and vibrant colours give this cushion a homespun Shaker appeal, and you can add as much or as little embroidery as you like to make it truly personal. The colourful pompons made with several strands of tapestry wools are extra speedy.*

### YOU WILL NEED

30 cm/12 in square of grey blanket
vanishing fabric marker
small piece of pink blanket
scrap fabric
fabric glue
tapestry needle
tapestry wools
cotton fabric for backing
two pieces of blanket in contrasting colours
sewing thread
card
press-and-close fastening or press fastener
30 cm-/12 in-square cushion pad

1 Trace off the heart template from the back of the book and cut it out. Place the template in the centre of the grey square and draw around it with the vanishing fabric marker.

2 Cut out the heart. Place the template on the pink blanket, draw around it and cut it out.

3 Place the pink heart in the cut-out area of the grey blanket, and glue a piece of scrap fabric behind the heart to hold it in place. Leave to dry.

4 Using the tapestry needle and wool, work straight stitch around the edge of the heart.

5 Embroider the heart with colourful cross stitches in tapestry wools.

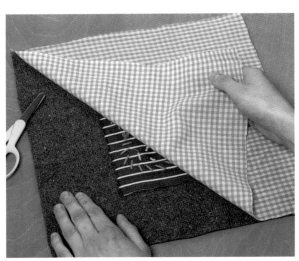

6 Cut a piece of backing fabric 30 cm/12 in square and place it on the back of the blanket appliqué.

7 Cut two cushion back pieces, each 30 x 20 cm/ 12 x 8 in, and embellish the edge of each piece with running stitch in a contrasting colour of thread (hem the edge first if not cut on a blanket selvedge). Place the two cushion backs on the cushion front, with right sides facing and back pieces overlapping. Tack in place. Machine stitch around the square with a 1 cm/½ in seam allowance. Turn the cover right side out, and press. Remove any visible tacking. ▶

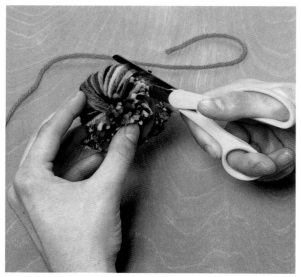

8 To make a pompon, cut two 5 cm/2 in diameter card rings with a 2.5 cm/1 in hole in the centre. Knot strands of tapestry wool on to the cards and wrap the wools around until the hole is full.

9 Insert the blade of a pair of scissors between the card rings and cut the wool. Tie a 30 cm/12 in length of wool between the card rings and tie in a knot. Remove the card and fluff up the pompon.

10 Make three more pompons the same size and sew one to each corner of the cushion. Sew a small piece of press-and-close fastening or a press fastener to the two opening edges of the cover. Insert the cushion pad and close the fastening.

# SCALLOPS AND BUTTONS

*Bring some colour to your couch with this vibrant scallop-edged cushion. Ours is made in needlecord, but you could use any closely woven fabric. Add embroidered self-cover buttons, or simply use large coloured buttons if you want to save time.*

### YOU WILL NEED
30 cm/12 in of 90 cm-/36 in-wide needlecord in each of three different colours
cord
masking tape
sewing thread
cotton embroidery threads
pinking shears
scraps of fabric for covering buttons
three self-cover buttons
button maker (optional)
40 x 26 cm/16 x 10 in cushion pad

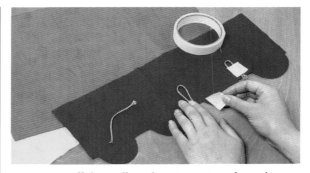

1 Trace off the scalloped pattern piece from the back of the book. From the needlecord, cut one back 42 x 28 cm/16½ x 11 in and one front 42 x 26 cm/16½ x 10 in. Using the scalloped pattern piece, cut two pieces for the border. Cut three 11 cm/4½ in lengths of cord and make each one into a loop. Place each loop in between the scallops, with the ends of the cord meeting the raw fabric edge. Secure them with masking tape.

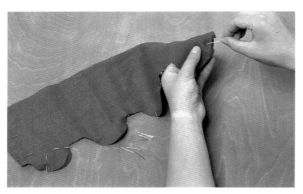

2 Place the two scallop-edged pieces of fabric together with right sides facing, and sew along the scalloped edge with a 1 cm/½ in seam allowance.

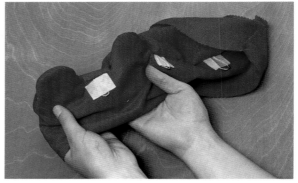

3 Turn right side out and then remove the masking tape. Press the fabric well.

▶

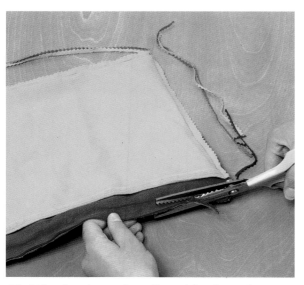

4 Hand sew a running stitch along the scalloped edge in a contrasting colour of embroidery thread. Make a narrow double hem on one long side of the cushion front.

5 Take the pieces of needlecord for the cushion front and back. Place the scalloped front on the cushion back with right sides facing, then place the hemmed cushion front on top, right side down. Tack, then machine stitch the edge with a 1 cm/½ in seam allowance. Snip the corners and trim the seams with pinking shears. Turn right side out and press.

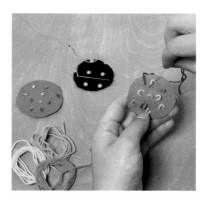

6 Cut three circles of fabric in different colours, 6 mm/¼ in larger than the buttons. Embellish each one with some embroidery stitches.

7 Cover each button using a button maker, or simply sew a running stitch around the edge of each circle and pull up the thread to gather the fabric. Press the button backs into position.

8 Sew the buttons on to the cover to correspond with the cord loops. Insert the cushion pad and then fasten the loops.

# SPOT ON

*Have fun creating your own spotted fabric design with fabric paints. Stick to just two or three complementary colours, or go for a jazzy, multi-coloured effect. If you are nervous about painting the spots freehand, practise them first on scrap paper.*

YOU WILL NEED
40 cm/16 in of 90 cm-/36 in-wide
white linen
30 cm/12 in of 90 cm-/36 in-wide
coloured linen
sewing thread
fabric paints
small paintbrush
cotton embroidery threads
selection of buttons
contrast fabric for the piping
1.8 m/2 yd piping cord
press-and-close fastening or
press fastener

1 Cut out two pieces of white linen: a 40 cm/16 in square for the front and a 42 x 22 cm/ 16½ x 9 in rectangle for the back. From coloured linen, cut a 42 x 30 cm/16½ x 12 in rectangle for the back. Fold over 1 cm/½ in of one edge of each back piece to make a hem, and stitch in place.

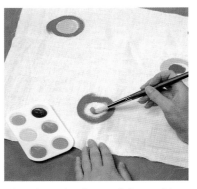

2 Place the front of the cushion on a flat covered surface and paint on different-coloured spots using fabric paints and the small paintbrush. Leave to dry.

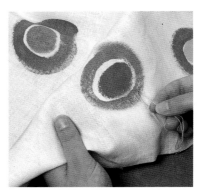

3 Decorate the spots with circles of running stitches in contrasting embroidery threads.

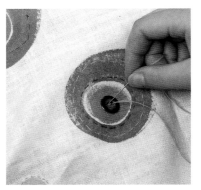

4 Sew a button in the centre of each of the spots.

5 Work a line of running stitch along the hem of the white cushion back.

▶

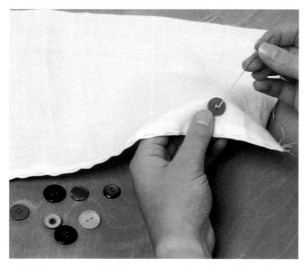

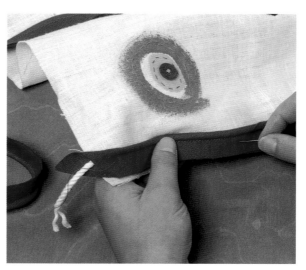

6 Sew a line of different-shaped and -coloured buttons above the running stitch. For the piping, cut 4 cm-/1½ in-wide bias strips of fabric and join them to make a 1.8 m-/2 yd-long strip. Fold this in half over the piping cord and stitch in place.

7 Pin the piping around the edge of the cushion front, with raw edges matching, and tack. Place the cushion backs on the cushion front with right sides facing. Using a zipper foot on the sewing machine, stitch the edges of the cushion close to the piping.

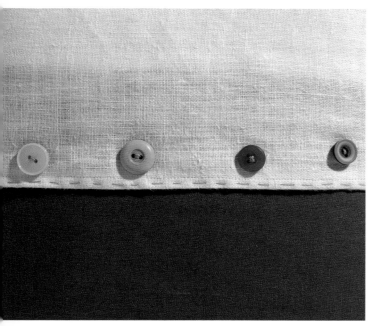

*Above: The different-coloured buttons on the back of the cushion continue the spotty theme.*

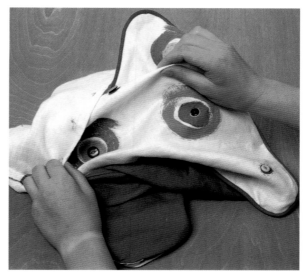

8 Snip the corners, then turn the cushion cover right side out and press. Sew a small piece of press-and-close fastening or a press fastener to the two opening edges of the cushion cover. Insert the cushion pad and close the fastening.

# TEA-TIME APPLIQUE

*Combine homely appliqué cups and saucers with linen tea-towels to create a simple cushion for the kitchen chair. Linen tea-towels come in a range of colours, so you can match the appliqué to suit your own colour scheme.*

YOU WILL NEED
2 linen tea-towels
fusible bonding web
scraps of blue fabric in different patterns
fine and soft-cotton embroidery threads
sewing thread
five 19 mm/¾ in self-cover buttons
button maker (optional)
40 x 26 cm/16 x 10 in cushion pad

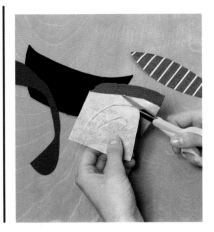

1 From the tea-towels, cut a front piece measuring 37 x 42cm/14½ x 16½ in, and two back pieces measuring 26 x 42 cm/10 x 16½ in and 28 x 42 cm/11 x 16½ in. Iron the bonding web on to the back of the scraps of blue fabric. Trace off the templates from the back of the book, and draw around them on to the bonding web. Cut out the teacup shapes.

2 Peel the backing paper from the bonding web, position the shapes on the front of the cushion fabric and iron in place.

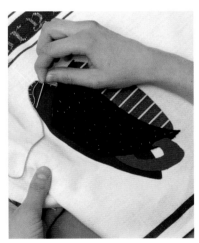

3 Embellish the cup and saucer with an assortment of simple stitches (see Techniques), using a mixture of fine and soft-cotton embroidery threads.

4 Cut a strip of fabric 55 x 4 cm/22 x 1½ in. Fold the strip in half widthways and press. Open out the fabric and fold the two sides into the centre and press, then fold in half.

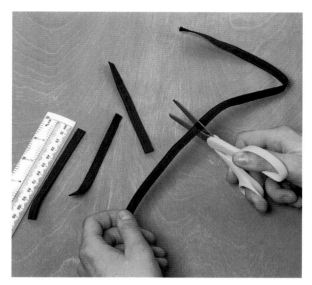

5 Sew along each side of the strip, then cut the strip into five 11 cm/4½ in lengths.

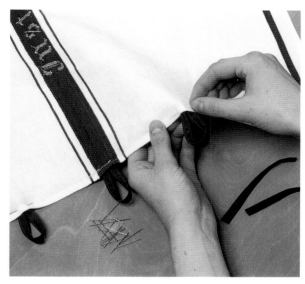

6 Fold each length in half to make a loop, and press. Position the loops along the long edge of one of the back pieces, on the wrong side. Tack in place and then stitch along the hem line.

7 Place the back piece with the loops on top of the appliqué, with right sides facing, then place the second piece on top. Tack and machine stitch around the edge with a 1 cm/½ in seam. Snip the corners, turn right side out and press. Remove the tacking.

8 To cover the buttons, cut five circles of blue fabric from the remaining scraps.

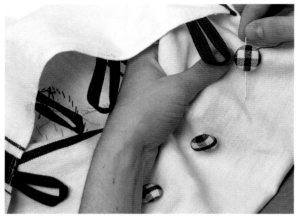

9 Cover each button using a button maker, or simply sew a running stitch around the edge of the circle and pull up the thread to gather the fabric. Press the backs of the buttons into position.

10 Sew the buttons on the back of the cushion to correspond with the button loops. Insert the cushion pad and fasten the loops.

*Right: The simple gingham buttons complete the country look of this kitchen cushion.*

# NAUTICAL NOTE

*Blue-and-white stripes and rope are two classic nautical themes – ideal for a bathroom or for a fresh seaside-inspired colour scheme. Our cushion is round, but the rope idea would work just as well on a square or rectangular cushion.*

YOU WILL NEED
large sheet of paper
sewing thread
drawing pin
pencil
60 cm/24 in of 137 cm-/54 in-wide striped canvas
tailor's chalk
twelve 15 mm/⅝ in eyelets and tool
hammer
45 cm-/18 in-diameter cushion pad
2 m/2¼ yd of 12 mm/½ in rope
strong off-white thread
press-and-close fastening or press fastener

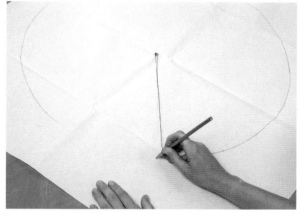

1 Draw a 53 cm-/21 in-diameter circle on paper using thread, a drawing pin and a pencil. Cut out.

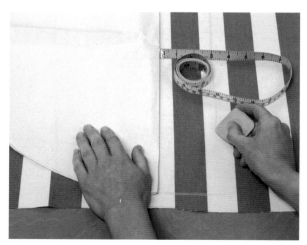

2 For the front, cut a circle of fabric, keeping the stripes equal on each side of the centre. For the back pieces, place the folded pattern on the fabric so that the stripes match the front piece. Add 7.5 cm/ 3 in to the straight edge and cut out, then repeat.

3 Fold under and tack a 2.5 cm/1 in hem along the straight edges of the back pieces. Stitch close to the hem edge and then top stitch. Overlap the two pieces to make a circle the same size as the front panel, and tack together along the straight edges. ▶

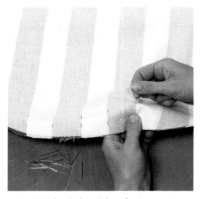

4 With right sides facing, pin the back and front together, matching the stripes carefully. Tack in position, then machine stitch with a 1.5 cm/⅝ in seam allowance. Remove the tacking.

5 Trim the seam allowance to 6 mm/¼ in. Snip notches around the edge and turn the cover right side out. Roll the seam between your fingers and tack close to the edge. Top stitch around the cover, 2.5 cm/1 in from the edge.

6 Fold the cover in four and, using tailor's chalk, mark the position of an eyelet in the middle of the border at each fold. Mark the positions of the other eyelets at equal intervals. Follow the manufacturer's instructions to insert an eyelet at each mark.

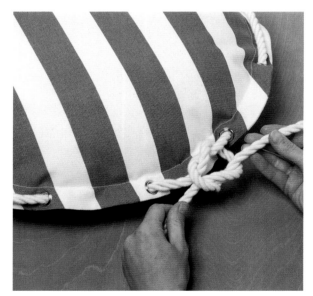

7 Insert the cushion pad and, beginning on the right side, thread the rope through the eyelets. Tie a reef knot by taking the left rope over the right rope and under, then the right rope over the left then under.

8 Whip the ends of the rope with the strong thread and sew in the ends securely. Cut the rope close to the whipping to finish. Sew a piece of press-and-close fastening or a press fastener to the overlapping edges on the back of the cushion cover.

# FLOWER POWER

*Big, bold, colourful flowers give this cushion a childlike simplicity. This is an ideal cushion for a beginner, as it is a simple square shape and the flowers are cut from a template. The self-cover buttons are easy to make, yet give a professional-looking finish.*

YOU WILL NEED
blanket in two contrasting colours
tapestry needle
wool threads
sewing thread
scraps of blanket
scraps of fine woollen fabric
nine 29 mm/1¼ in self-cover buttons
button maker (optional)
press-and-close fastening or press fastener
60 cm-/24 in-square cushion pad

1 Measure and cut out three pieces of blanket: a 60 cm/24 in square for the front, and two 60 x 40 cm/24 x 16 in pieces for the back. Embellish the edges of the cushion backs with running stitch in a contrasting-coloured wool thread (hem the edges first if not cut on a blanket selvedge).

2 Place the two back pieces of blanket on the cushion front, with right sides facing. Pin in place and sew together around the edge with a 1 cm/½ in seam allowance. Snip the corners, turn the cover right side out and press.

3 Work blanket stitch (see Techniques) around the edge of the cushion, using a different-coloured wool for each side.

▶

25

4 Trace off the flower template from the back of the book. Draw around it, and cut out nine flowers from the scraps of blanket.

5 Position the flowers on the blanket square in a grid, and pin them in place.

6 Cut nine circles of coloured fine woollen fabric to cover the buttons.

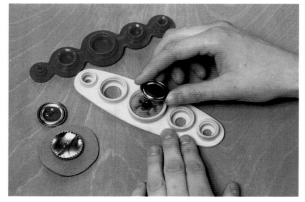

7 Cover the buttons (see step 7 on page 14), and press the backs of the buttons into position.

8 Sew a button to the centre of each flower. Sew a small piece of press-and-close fastening or a press fastener to the opening edges of the cushion. Insert the cushion pad and close the fastening.

# PATCHWORK VELVET PINCUSHION

*In Victorian times, pincushions were sewn to commemorate births, christenings, weddings and St Valentine's Day. This small patchwork of velvets, trimmed with gold braid and decorated with brass pins, would make a lovely gift for a dressmaker.*

YOU WILL NEED
scraps of velvet in yellow, pink, green and brown
sewing thread
polyester stuffing
narrow gold braid
brass lace-making pins
four yellow ribbon roses
fray-resist glue
fabric glue
small gold beads

1 From velvet, cut one 10 cm/4 in yellow square, four 7.5 cm/3 in pink squares and four 7.5 x 10 cm/3 x 4 in green rectangles. With right sides facing and with a 1 cm/½ in seam allowance, sew the pieces into three strips: join a pink square to each of the short ends of the two green rectangles, and stitch the other two green rectangles to opposite sides of the yellow square.

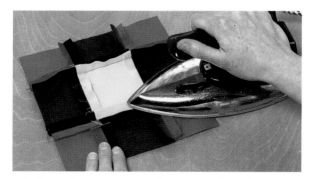

2 Press the seams open, then pin and stitch one narrow strip to either side of the wide strip. Do not worry if the joins are not precisely accurate, as they will be covered by the gold braid. Press the two long seams open.

3 Cut a 20 cm/8 in square of brown velvet, and pin it to the patchwork square with right sides facing. Seam around the outside edge, leaving a gap of about 5 cm/2 in gap on one side. Clip the corners, turn right side out and fill with stuffing. Close the opening with slip stitch. ▶

4 Attach gold braid around the centre square with brass pins, mitring the corners (see Techniques).

5 Pin a yellow ribbon rose to each corner of the centre square.

6 Trace the heart template from the back of the book on to thin paper, and cut out. Draw around the heart on the wrong side of a piece of pink velvet, and coat the pencil line with a thin layer of fray-resist glue. Allow to dry, then cut out.

7 Fix the heart on the centre square with a light layer of fabric glue. When this is dry, use brass pins to attach small gold beads all the way around the outside edge of the heart.

# CARPE DIEM

*"Carpe Diem" means literally "seize the day". You may feel slightly guilty as you recline on the sofa with this invigorating motto, but no matter. Help yourself to another chocolate and resolve to seize the day tomorrow.*

### YOU WILL NEED

50 cm/20 in of 115 cm-/45 in-wide scoured linen, prewashed
soft pencil
masking tape
embroidery hoop
embroidery needle
stranded embroidery cotton in mushroom brown
2 m/2¼ yd of 1cm/½ in antique-gold flat braid
30 x 40 cm/12 x 16 in cushion pad

1 Cut a piece of fabric 33 x 43 cm/13 x 17 in for the cushion front. Trace off the template from the back of the book. Using a soft pencil, draw thickly over the lines of the motto on the reverse side of the tracing paper.

2 Position the tracing centrally on the front piece of linen, and secure it with masking tape. Draw over the outline to transfer the design to the fabric.

3 Place the fabric in the embroidery hoop, and then embroider a clear outline to each letter using back stitch.

31

4 To emphasize the scrolled parts of each letter, whip the back stitch, passing around the back stitches only (not through the fabric beneath).

5 Fill in the solid parts of the letters, using long and short stitches worked in a vertical direction within each letter.

6 Work satin stitch across each letter, forming a smooth, slightly padded horizontal surface which covers the long and short stitches. Take care gradually to adjust the angle of the satin stitch as you follow the curves of each letter, to produce a flowing, script-like form.

7 To make up the cushion cover, cut two back pieces 33 x 28 cm/13 x 11 in. Make a narrow double hem on one long edge of each back piece. Overlap the back pieces, pin them to the cushion front with right sides facing and raw edges matching. Machine stitch making a 1 cm/½ in seam.

For the border, cut two strips 23 x 56 cm/9 x 22½ in. Fold each border strip in half lengthways and, starting 1.5 cm/⅝ in from the edge of the fold, draw a line at a 45° angle to the raw edges of the strip. Unfold and pin the four border pieces together along the marked lines to make a rectangle. Stitch seams. Trim the seam allowances to 1.5 cm/⅝ in. Press seams open and turn border right side out.

With right sides together, pin the back edge of the border to the back of the cushion cover, matching raw edges and corners. Tack then machine in place, pivoting the work on the needle at the corners. Press turnings towards the border.

Fold the border in half and pin the front edge to the cushion front. Slip stitch in place, through the first line of stitching. Pin the flat braid over the slip stitching and hand sew in place, folding the braid neatly at the corners to form mitres.

# TAKE A SEAT

*Make a ribbon-trimmed seat cushion for a favourite chair. Match the colour of the fabric and ribbons to your tablecloth or garden parasol to create a co-ordinating set. If you want a more fitted cushion, make a paper pattern of your chair seat and use this to cut out the fabric.*

YOU WILL NEED
80 cm/32 in of 137 cm-/54 in-wide fabric
225 g/8 oz polyester wadding
sewing thread
vanishing fabric marker
5 m/5½ yd each of 2 mm/⅛ in embroidery ribbon in six different
shades (blue, green and yellow)
large needle
7.5 cm/3 in square of stiff card
two 1 cm/ ½ in wooden beads

1 Cut two 45 cm/18 in squares of fabric and wadding, and place a fabric square on top of each wadding square. Work lines of tacking, radiating out from the centre, to hold the two layers together.

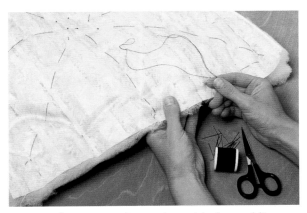

2 Pin the two panels together with the wadding inside, and tack securely around each side 2.5 cm/1 in from the edge.

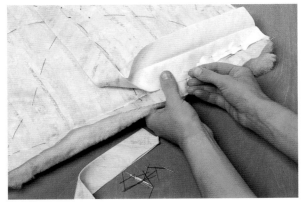

3 Cut four 7.5 cm-/3 in-wide bias strips, about 50 cm/20 in long, from the remaining fabric, and press to remove some of the stretch. Press in half lengthways. Pin, tack and stitch the bias strips along the edges of the cushion, keeping the edge of each strip along the tacked line.

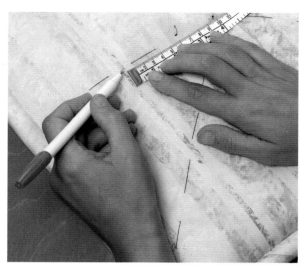

4 Trim the wadding and fabric to the edge of the binding. Fold the binding to the back, turn it under and pin. Mitre the corners and trim away any excess fabric before slip stitching. Slip stitch the rest of the binding. Remove any visible tacking.

5 Mark the centre of the cushion on the right side with the vanishing fabric marker, and then measure out from the centre to make a grid of nine marks, each 10 cm/4 in apart.

6 Thread 20 cm/8 in lengths of ribbon on to a needle. Insert the needle through the cushion at one of the marks, leaving 5 cm/2 in of ends on the right side. Bring the needle back up and go through the same holes, leaving the ends on the right side.

7 Pull the ribbons tightly and tie securely. Trim the ends to 2 cm/¾ in. Repeat at the other eight marks.

▶

8 Wrap all six colours of ribbon around the stiff card six times. Cut the ends, then thread a single length of ribbon underneath the ribbons and tie securely. Snip the ribbons off the card and press to remove the creases.

9 Place a wooden bead under the tie and pull the ribbons down to cover it. Tie a second length of single ribbon around the ribbons to form the neck of the tassel, and tie securely. Trim the ends neatly. Make another tassel to match, and stitch them on to the front corners of the cushion.

10 Cut two bundles of 30 cm/12 in lengths of ribbon. Wrap a single length of ribbon around the centre of each bundle to hold the ribbons in place. Stitch these central ribbons to the back corners of the cushion and knot the ribbons. Tie the ribbons around the back of the chair.

*Above: A more fitted cushion is just as easy to make, and looks very stylish on a simple kitchen chair.*

# FRINGED VELVET

*Do you have a collection of fabric remnants and trimmings hidden away in a cupboard? If so, bring them out and transform them into a sumptuous patchwork cushion that will grace any sofa. Try furnishing-fabric departments as sources of beautiful fringes and trimmings.*

YOU WILL NEED
50 cm/20 in of 115 cm-/36 in-wide velvet for cushion back
sewing thread
40 cm/16 in zip
card
40 cm/16 in square of each of red, green and grey velvet
pinking shears
80 cm/32 in beaded fringing
60 x 40 cm/24 x 16 in cushion pad

1 For the cushion back, cut one piece of velvet 43 x 8 cm/17 x 3¼ in and one piece 58 x 43 cm/23 x 17 in. Join the two pieces, inserting a zip in the centre of the seam (see Techniques). Make a card template for a triangle from the back of the book. Cut out a triangle from red velvet, using pinking shears. Cut out a grey velvet triangle in the same way, then turn the template over and cut out another grey and red triangle. Cut two green velvet triangles, then turn the template over and cut out two more. Pin a green and a red triangle right sides together along the diagonal edges. Machine stitch with a 1.5 cm/⅝ in seam and repeat for the three other pairs of triangles.

2 Pin two patched rectangles right sides facing along their longest edges, matching diagonal seams. Machine stitch with a 1.5 cm/⅝ in seam.

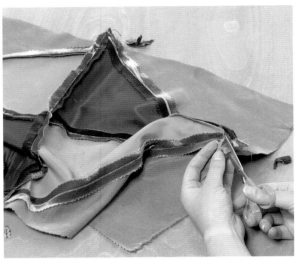

3 Pin the two front halves of the cushion together, carefully matching the centre seams, and machine stitch with a 1.5 cm/⅝ in seam.

4 Press the seams open, and trim down the seam allowances to reduce the bulk of fabric.

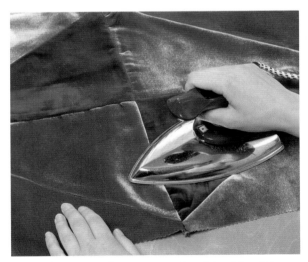

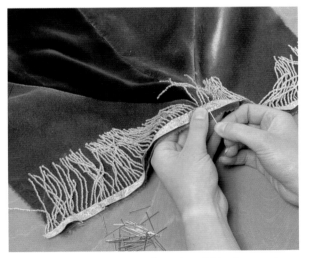

5 Lightly press the seams on the right side of the patchwork, using a cool iron.

6 Cut two 40 cm/16 in lengths of fringing, and pin one to each short edge of the cushion front. Machine stitch in place, using a zipper foot to avoid breaking the beads. With the zip open and right sides facing, pin and machine stitch the cushion front and back together with a 1.5 cm/⅝ in seam. Clip the corners and turn the cover right side out. Insert the cushion pad and close the zip.

# PERSONALLY YOURS

*Perfect as a christening gift or to celebrate the birth of a baby, this delicate cushion in fresh gingham and broderie anglaise has timeless appeal. Photocopy your chosen initials — calligraphy books are always a good source of attractive lettering — ready to transfer to the fabric.*

### YOU WILL NEED

12.5 cm/5 in square of 12-count
aida fabric
sewing thread
soft pencil
stranded embroidery thread
vanishing fabric marker
15 x 17 cm/6 x 6½ in gingham
33 cm/13 in narrow white broderie
anglaise edging
1.5 m/1¾ yd of 10 cm-/4 in-wide broderie
anglaise edging
15 x 17 cm/6 x 7 in white backing fabric
polyester stuffing
pot-pourri
four buttons

1 Find the centre of the aida fabric by folding it in half each way and tacking along the creases. Transfer your chosen initials to the fabric (see steps 1 and 2 on page 31), and sew them in cross stitch so that one initial lies on each side of the central line.

2 Cut a 10 cm/4 in square of paper. Place this diagonally on the embroidery so that one corner lies on each tacked line. Draw around it with a vanishing fabric marker and cut out the diamond shape.

3 Pin and stitch the diamond shape to the centre of the gingham. Slip stitch the narrow broderie anglaise around the diamond, mitring it neatly at the corners (see Techniques).

4 Join the wide broderie anglaise to make a circle. Fold this into four, and mark the quarters with notches on the top edge. Make four lines of gathering stitches, by hand or machine, between the notches (see Techniques).

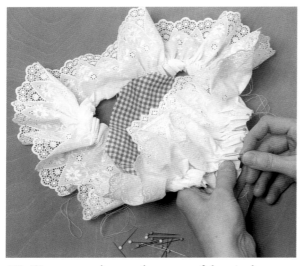

5 Pin one notch to each corner of the gingham, so that the lace lies towards the centre. Draw up the gathering threads so that the frill fits along each side, and knot the thread ends. Distribute the gathers evenly, allowing a little more fullness at each corner. Pin and tack in place.

6 Pin the gathers to the gingham, so that they do not get caught in the stitching. With right sides facing, pin the gingham front to the white backing fabric. Stitch them together 1 cm/½ in from the edge, leaving a 5 cm/2 in gap on one side.

7 Clip the corners and turn the cover right side out. Stuff with stuffing and pot-pourri, then slip stitch the opening closed.

8 Finish by sewing a button on to each corner of the cushion with embroidery thread.

# SILVER TOUCH

*Silver machine embroidery and glitzy metallic organza combine beautifully with grey velvet to make a rich cushion. Practise the fluid machine embroidery on spare fabric before trying it out on the velvet. The hoop is important for holding the fabric taut and moving it around.*

YOU WILL NEED
50 cm/20 in of 90 cm-/36 in-wide grey velvet
vanishing fabric marker
embroidery hoop
silver machine-embroidery thread
20 cm/8 in of 90 cm-/36 in-wide pleated metallic organza
sewing thread
40 cm/16 in zip
40 cm-/16 in-square cushion pad

1 For the cushion front, cut a piece of velvet 43 cm/17 in square. Using the vanishing fabric marker, draw wavy guidelines for the embroidery. Place the fabric in the embroidery hoop. Select a free-embroidery or darning mode on the sewing machine and attach a darning foot. Stitch the design using the silver machine-embroidery thread.

2 Cut a strip of metallic organza 170 x 5 cm/ 67 x 2 in, joining strips as necessary. With raw edges matching, fold the strip in half lengthways, pin, tack and machine stitch along the raw edges. For the cushion back, cut one piece of velvet 43 x 35 cm/17 x 14 in and one piece 43 x 11 cm/17 x 4½ in. Stitch the zip in the seam with a 1.5 cm/⅝ in allowance.

3 Pin the organza frill around the embroidered cushion front, joining the ends as for piping (see Techniques). Machine stitch. With right sides facing and the zip open, pin the cushion front and back together. Stitch around the edge with a 1.5 cm/⅝ in seam allowance. Clip the corners and turn right side out. Insert the cushion pad and close the zip.

# ORGANZA DUO

*A metallic-organza cover slipped over a satin cushion makes a theatrical combination.*
*When choosing the fabrics, hold the organza over the satin to see how the colours*
*affect one another when they are combined.*

YOU WILL NEED
50 cm/20 in of 90 cm-/36 in-wide satin
sewing thread
press fasteners
38 cm-/15 in-square cushion pad
1 m/1 yd of 115 cm-/45 in-wide metallic organza
tailor's chalk
ruler

1 For the front, cut a 42 cm/16½ in square of satin and for the back cut two pieces 42 x 23 cm/ 16½ x 9½ in. Turn, press and stitch a 1 cm/½ in double hem on one long edge of each back piece. Pin and stitch the cushion front and back together, with right sides facing and back pieces overlapping.

2 Clip the corners and turn right side out. On the opening edges of the back, mark and stitch pairs of press fasteners at even intervals. Insert the cushion pad and close the fasteners.

3 For the organza cover, cut one 51 cm/20¼ in square for the front and two 51 x 28 cm/20¼ x 11 in pieces for the back. Turn and press a double 1 cm/½ in hem on one long edge of each back piece. Assemble and stitch together as for the satin cover, with a 1.5 cm/⅝ in seam allowance. ▶

4 Trim away the seam allowance to 6 mm/¼ in from the stitching, and clip the corners. Turn the cover right side out, and top stitch 6 mm/¼ in from the folded edge. On the cushion front, mark a line 5 cm/2 in from the edge all around, using tailor's chalk and a ruler. Machine stitch along the line.

5 On the opening edges of the cover back, mark and stitch pairs of press fasteners at intervals. Insert the satin cushion and fasten the organza cover.

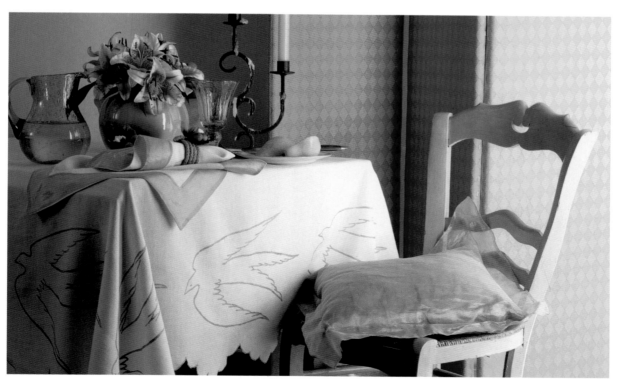

*Above: On this cushion the pad is covered with bright satin and the impact is diffused by a second cover of translucent fabric.*

# HEARTS AND FLOWERS

*A heart is a pleasing shape, whether for Valentine's Day or all year round. Go overboard with this one in silk and velvet, and trim it with an ornate silk rose. Make a whole selection of cushions and pile them up at the head of your bed for a touch of glamour.*

YOU WILL NEED
heart-shaped cushion pad
graph paper
card
50 cm/20 in of 115 cm-/45 in-wide lilac silk dupion
50 cm/20 in of 115 cm-/45 in-wide green velvet
piping cord
matching thread
18 cm/7 in zip
20 cm/8 in blue silk dupion
tailor's chalk
self-cover button
button maker (optional)

1 To make a card template, first press one half of the cushion pad on to a piece of graph paper and draw around the edge. Mark a line 2 cm/¾ in outside the first, and cut around this second line. Place the paper pattern on a folded piece of card and draw around it. Cut the card template and open it out.

2 Cut out one heart in lilac silk and one in green velvet. Measure around one heart and cut a piece of piping cord to this measurement plus 6 cm/2½ in. Cut a 4 cm-/1½ in-wide bias strip from green velvet and cover the piping cord, using a zipper foot. Pin the piping around the lilac-silk cushion front, and stitch in place using a piping or a zipper foot.

3 With right sides facing, pin and machine stitch the cushion front and back together with a 2 cm/¾ in seam and leaving an 18 cm/7 in gap in one straight edge for the zip. Clip the seam allowance and turn the cover right side out. Hand sew the zip into the piped seam (see Techniques).

▶

4 Draw a petal shape and enlarge it to three different sizes. Fold the blue silk dupion in half and draw four large, five medium and four small petal shapes with the tailor's chalk. Carefully cut out the petals through the double layer of silk, adding 6 mm/¼ in all around.

5 Machine stitch the petals in pairs along the marked lines, leaving the bottom edge of each unstitched. Turn the petals right side out and press.

6 Select a long stitch on the sewing machine. Stitch along the bottom edges of the largest petal shapes, then progress to the medium and lastly to the smallest petal shapes, without breaking off the thread in between. Secure the threads at one end and then, drawing on the top thread only, carefully pull up the gathers along the string of petals.

7 Arrange the petals, starting with the largest and spiralling the string around a central point. Pin in place. Stab stitch to secure (see Techniques), and stitch to the top of the cushion front.

8 Draw around a self-cover button on the wrong side of some green velvet, adding a 6 mm/¼ in seam allowance. Cover the button using a button maker, or sew a running stitch around the edge of the velvet circle and pull up the thread to gather the fabric. Press the back of the button into place. Stitch the button to the centre of the rose to cover the raw edges. Insert the cushion pad and close the zip.

# PINK PERFECTION

*An extravagant patchwork of toning shades of silk makes this a luxury cushion. The edges are padded for added opulence. If pink is not your colour, look for remnants of silk dupion in jewel-bright colours such as jade, burnt orange or peacock blue.*

YOU WILL NEED
paper
ruler
vanishing fabric marker
50 cm/20 in of 115 cm/45 in-wide silk dupion in each of
red, lilac and pink
sewing thread
polyester wadding
press-and-close fastening or press fastener
45 cm-/18 in-square cushion pad

1 Cut a piece of paper 48 cm/19 in square for a template. Fold this in half diagonally and in half diagonally again, then unfold it and cut out the four triangles. Draw around these templates with vanishing fabric marker, and cut out four triangles in red silk and four in lilac. Pin one red and one lilac triangle together, with right sides facing. Machine stitch along the two short edges with a 1.5 cm/⅝ in seam. Clip the seams. Assemble the other triangles in the same way. Turn right side out and press.

2 Cut a 48 cm/19 in square pink–silk cushion front. Place right side up on a table, and arrange the triangles with the lilac side facing down and with the unseamed edges matching the sides of the square. Pin in place. Pin the points of the triangles in place where they meet. Fold back the two shorter edges of the triangle to reveal the lilac side, and pin.

3 Top stitch the triangles to the cushion front 2 mm/⅛ in from the edge.

▶

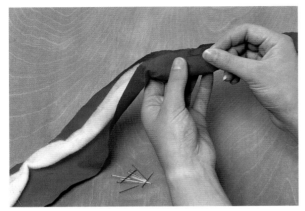

4 Cut a strip of wadding 2 m x 5 cm/2¼ yd x 2 in, joining as necessary. Cut a 2 m-/2¼ yd-long x 7.5 cm-/3 in-wide bias strip of pink silk, and place it on a table, with the right side down. Roll up the wadding and place it along the centre of the strip. Pin the fabric evenly around the wadding.

5 Machine stitch along the strip to complete the piping, using a zipper foot. With raw edges matching, pin the piping all around the cushion front and then machine stitch.

6 For the cushion back, cut two pieces of red silk 48 x 30 cm/19 x 12 in. Turn and press a 2 cm/ ¾ in double hem on one long edge of each piece. Pin and machine stitch in place. Place the cushion front and backs together with right sides facing and the back pieces overlapping. Pin and machine stitch in place. Turn the cover right side out and sew a small piece of press-and-close fastening or a press fastener to the opening edges. Insert the cushion pad and then close the fastening.

# GREY SILK TRELLIS

*The unusual fringing made from the main silk fabric is easy to sew, and yet looks really effective. Choose toning buttons to hold the trelliswork in place and for fastening the rouleau loops on the back. Finish with a tassel at each corner, made from the same silk dupion.*

YOU WILL NEED
55 cm/20 in of 115 cm-/45 in-wide grey silk dupion
sewing thread
23 shell buttons
blunt needle or safety pin
four 15 mm/⅝ in cotton balls
55 x 30 cm/22 x 12 in cushion pad

1 For the cushion front, cut a piece of grey silk 58 x 33 cm/23 x 13 in. For the trelliswork, cut several strips of silk 2.5 cm/1 in wide. On each strip fold one long edge over by 1 cm/½ in, and top stitch 2 mm/⅛ in from the folded edge. Using a needle, carefully separate and remove the threads from both raw edges, pulling away the threads right up to the seamline to make a fringe.

2 Arrange the frayed strips on the cushion front in a lattice pattern, with the parallel strips placed 11 cm/4½ in apart.

3 Sew a button at each of the intersections, then stitch all around the edge of the fabric to hold the strips in position.

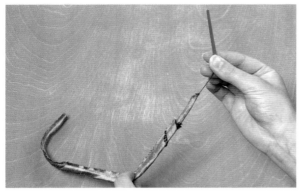

4 To make the rouleau loops, cut a strip of fabric 33 x 3 cm/13 x 1¼ in. Fold in half lengthways with right sides together, and machine stitch 6 mm/ ¼ in from the folded edge. Attach a thread to one end and pass the strip through the eye of a blunt needle or a safety pin, then push the needle or safety pin through the tube to turn the loop right side out. Cut the strip into three 11 cm/4½ in lengths. For the cushion back, cut one piece of fabric 20 x 33 cm/ 8 x 13 in and one piece 51 x 33 cm/20¼ x 13 in.

5 On the smaller back piece, turn and press a 2 cm-/¾ in-wide double hem on one long edge. On one short edge of the larger piece, position and pin the three rouleau loops, checking that the loops will fit over the buttons. Tack and machine stitch the loops in place. Cut a facing 33 x 5 cm/13 x 2 in, and neaten one long edge. With right sides together, pin and machine stitch the facing over the rouleau loops. Turn and press the facing to the wrong side and then top stitch.

6 With right sides facing and raw edges matching, place the larger back piece on the front piece. Place the smaller back piece on top, with the right side facing down and raw edges matching. Sew the cover around all four sides and turn through. Sew on buttons to match the loops. For each tassel, cut two pieces of fabric 10 cm/4 in square. Sew zigzag stitch 1.5 cm/⅝ in from the raw edges. Fray the edges (see Step 1), pulling away threads up to the stitched line.

7 Mark a 5 cm-/2 in-diameter circle in the centre of the square. Run a gathering thread along the marked line. Place a cotton ball in the centre, draw up the gathers and secure them, then wind the thread around the gathering thread and secure with a stitch. Insert the needle inside the cotton ball and bring it out at the top of the tassel, then stitch to one corner of the cushion. Repeat to make three more tassels. Insert the cushion pad and fasten the rouleau loops.

# STITCH IN TIME

*These two stylish covers are both suitable for beginners to tackle. The dark woollen square is simply embroidered with three rows of running stitch around the edge. The white-cord trim and toggle fastenings on both cushions add to their chunky appeal.*

### EMBROIDERED CUSHION

YOU WILL NEED
50 cm/20 in of 115 cm-/45 in-wide grey woollen fabric
white perle embroidery thread
embroidery needle
sewing thread
pinking shears
2 m/2¼ yd white cord
vanishing fabric marker
three toggles
45 cm-/18 in-square cushion pad

1 For the cushion front, cut a 48 cm/19 in square of fabric. Mark a line 7.5 cm/3 in from the edge all round. Work a running stitch in embroidery thread along the marked line, then work two more parallel lines 1 cm/½ in apart inside the marked line.

2 For the cushion back, use pinking shears to cut one piece of fabric 18 x 48 cm/7 x 19 in and another 44 x 48 cm/17½ x 19 in. Neaten the opening edges and turn under by 5 cm/2 in. Pin, and machine stitch 2 mm/⅛ in and then 2 cm/¾ in from the folded edge. Work three rows of running stitch in embroidery thread along both edges.

3 Assemble the cushion front and backs with right sides facing and the back pieces overlapping. Pin and machine stitch around the edge with a 1 cm/½ in seam and leaving a 10 cm/4 in gap in one side. Clip the corners, turn right side out and press. Push one end of the cord into the opening in the seam, and stab stitch in place along the seam (see Techniques).

4 At each corner of the cover, carefully twist the cord into a small loop, then continue along the next seam.

5 Push the other end of the cord into the opening in the seam, overlapping the two ends slightly. Stab stitch in place and slip stitch the opening closed.

6 Mark the positions of three toggles at equal distances on the underlap of the cushion back. Mark the corresponding positions for the loops on the overlap, using a vanishing fabric marker. At the edge of the overlap work three or four large stitches over one finger in embroidery thread, in each marked position, ensuring that these threads will fit easily over the toggles.

7 Then work a tight blanket stitch along the threads to hold them together (see Techniques). Make a small stitch in the fabric to finish off. Stitch the toggles in place and insert the cushion pad.

## FRINGED CUSHION

YOU WILL NEED

20 cm/8 in woollen fabric in each of green, burgundy and red

30 cm/12 in grey-blue woollen fabric

pinking shears

sewing thread

pink embroidery thread

embroidery needle

four toggles

40 cm-/16 in-square cushion pad

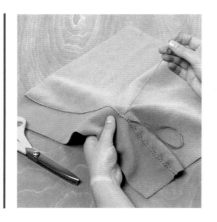

1 For the cushion back, cut one piece of green fabric 13 x 43 cm/5¼ x 17 in and a piece of grey-blue fabric 33 x 43 cm/13 x 17 in, using pinking shears. Lap the grey-blue fabric over the green by 3 cm/1¼ in, and top stitch 1 cm/½ in from the pinked edge. Using pink embroidery thread, work a line of running stitch along the machine-stitched line. ▶

2 To make a pinked fringe, cut two 170 cm/67 in fabric strips, one in burgundy 3 cm/ 1¼ in wide and one in green 4 cm/1½ in wide. Place the strips together, matching one long edge of each, and then pin and machine stitch down the centre. Trim the long edges of the burgundy fabric to 1 cm/½ in and the green to 1.5 cm/⅝ in from the stitched line.

3 Arrange the fringing around the right side of the cushion back. Pin and machine stitch in place. For the cushion front, cut a piece of red fabric 13 x 43 cm/ 5¼ x 17 in, a piece of burgundy fabric 20 x 43 cm/8 x 17 in and a piece of grey-blue fabric 26 x 43 cm/10 x 17 in.

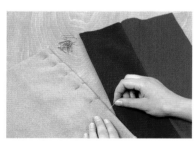

4 Join the red and burgundy pieces by the longest edges. Neaten the opening edges of the front pieces and fold under by 5 cm/2 in. Pin and machine stitch 2 cm/¾ in from the folded edge. Work a running stitch with pink embroidery thread along the machine-stitched line.

5 Assemble the cushion pieces with right sides together, and overlapping the grey-blue underside piece. Pin and machine stitch together with a 1 cm/½ in seam. Clip the corners and turn right side out. On the underlap, mark the toggle positions. On the overlap, mark the positions of the loops. Make four loops as in step 6 of the Embroidered Cushion. Insert the cushion pad and fasten the toggles.

# RIBBON WEAVING

*Ribbons come in such a wonderful array of colours, widths and textures that you can thoroughly indulge yourself by making this cushion. Only short lengths of ribbon are needed, so add end-of-roll bargains to your own workbasket collection to make up the amount.*

YOU WILL NEED
50 cm/20 in of 90 cm-/36 in-wide calico
sewing thread
40 cm/16 in zip
fusible bonding web
selection of ribbons
1.7 m/2 yd piping cord
50 cm/20 in satin
40 cm-/16 in-square cushion pad

1 For the cushion front, cut a piece of calico 43 cm/17 in square. For the back, cut two pieces of satin 43 x 23 cm/17 x 9½ in. Join the two back pieces together, inserting a zip in the seam. Cut a piece of fusible bonding web 43 cm/17 in square and press face down on the calico. Peel away the backing paper from the bonding web.

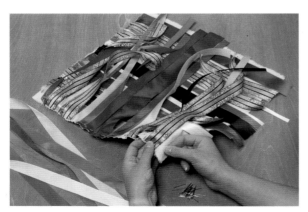

2 Cut the ribbons into 43 cm/17 in lengths. Pin the ribbons to two adjacent sides of the calico, 1 cm/½ in from the edges.

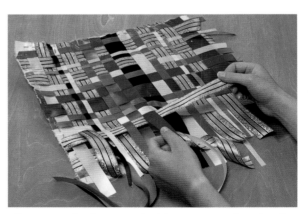

3 Weave the horizontal ribbons over and under the vertical ribbons, pulling them taut. Pin them in place at the other end.

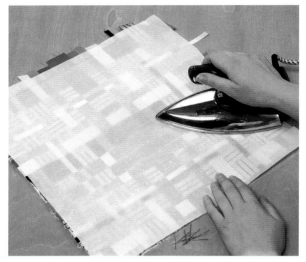

4 Turn the calico over and, using a hot iron, press the calico to fuse the woven ribbons in place.

5 To make the ruched piping to go around the edges of the cushion, cut 4 cm-/1½ in-wide bias strips of satin to twice the length of the piping cord, joining the strips as necessary.

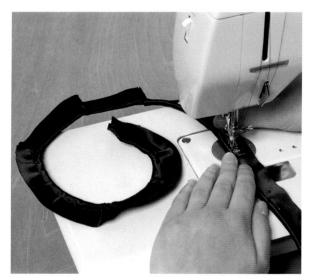

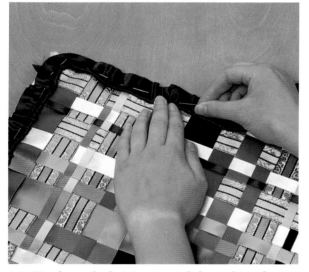

6 Fold the bias binding in half around the piping cord, and pin. Secure the cord at one end, then machine stitch along it for 30 cm/12 in. Raise the foot, leaving the needle in the fabric. Pull the cord through the fabric tube to gather the fabric. Repeat along the length of the piping and secure at the end.

7 Pin the ruched piping around the cushion front, and stitch. Place the cushion back on top, and pin into position. With right sides facing and the zip open, machine stitch all around the seam. Clip the corners and turn the cover right side out. Insert the cushion pad and close the zip.

# COUNTRY CHECK

*Patchwork and gingham go together like strawberries and cream. The patchwork front is machine-stitched for speed and strength, then hand-finished with traditional quilting knots. The cover is completed with simple ties to fasten the back.*

YOU WILL NEED
card
selection of gingham fabrics
50 cm/20 in of 90 cm-/45 cm-wide calico
sewing thread
string
drawing pin
pencil
paper
white perle embroidery thread
tapestry needle
40 cm-/16 in-diameter cushion pad

1 Make a card template 11 cm/4½ in square. Draw around the template on to the gingham fabric and add a 1 cm/½ in seam allowance. Cut out 16 squares. Pin these together in pairs, with right sides facing. Stitch along one edge with a 1 cm/½ in seam allowance. Join the pairs into strips of four squares. Press the seams open.

2 Join two strips together along one long edge, taking care to match the seams.

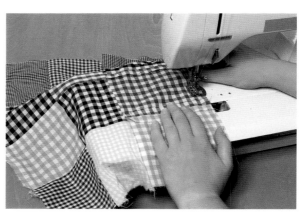

3 Continue adding the strips to form a large square. Press the seams open. ▶

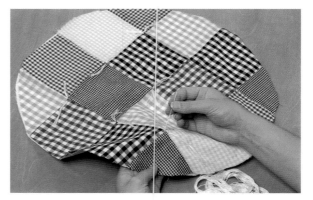

4 Using the string, drawing pin and pencil, draw a 43 cm-/17 in-diameter circle on paper. Cut this out, and use it to cut a circle of calico and a circle of patchwork for the cushion front. Place the patched piece wrong side down on the calico. Tack around the edge to hold the two layers together.

5 Thread the tapestry needle with several lengths of embroidery thread. Insert the needle at the corners of the patches, leaving an end of 4 cm/1½ in. Make a stitch and bring the needle back through to the right side of the fabric.

6 Tie the strands in a knot and trim. Remove the tacking. For the cushion back, fold the paper template vertically into four. Cut along one fold line to make one large and one small template. Cut the two back pieces from calico, adding 2.5 cm/1 in to each straight edge. Cut two facings 5 cm/2 in wide and neaten one long edge of each. Pin one facing to the smaller back piece, with right sides facing. Stitch the seam, turn and press. Stitch a hem, 2 mm/⅛ in and 2 cm/¾ in from the seamed edge.

7 Make six ties from 10 x 18 cm/4 x 7 in pieces of gingham (see Techniques). Position three ties at equal intervals along the opening edge of the larger back piece, matching the raw edges, and machine stitch. Pin the second facing to the opening edge, over the ties and with right sides facing, and machine stitch. Turn and fold the facing to the wrong side. Machine stitch the hem, as in step 6.

8 On the back underlap, mark the corresponding positions of the other three ties. Turn under the raw edge of each remaining tie and pin in place. Top stitch in an "X" pattern. Pin the cushion front to the backs with right sides facing, and machine stitch around the edge with a 1.5 cm/⅝ in seam. Clip the seam allowances all round. Turn right side out, insert the cushion pad and fasten the ties.

# NATURAL CUSHIONS

*Each of these natural finishes brings a touch of individuality to purchased, ready-made cushion covers, with a minimal outlay of effort and expense. Display one cushion on its own, or pile all three together on one chair for a comfortable and homely look.*

YOU WILL NEED
natural-coloured cushion covers
sewing thread

SEA-SHELL BORDER
old shell necklace
larger sea shells
drill and 1.5 mm/¹⁄₁₆ in high-speed
steel drill bit

SOFT-CORD APPLIQUÉ
6 mm/¼ in natural cotton piping cord
small safety pins

ROSE APPLIQUÉ WITH RAFFIA TASSELS
raffia
builder's brick line
sisal rope
buttons (optional)

## SEA-SHELL BORDER

1 Remove the shells from the necklace string. Place the larger shells on a firm surface, and very carefully drill a hole in each.

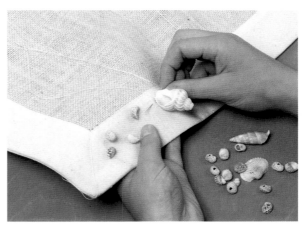

2 Stitch the shells randomly in place around the border of the cushion, taking care to secure with additional back stitches every few shells.

## SOFT-CORD APPLIQUÉ

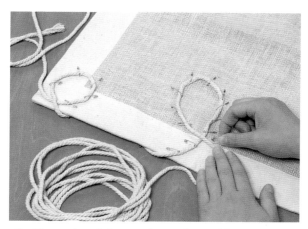

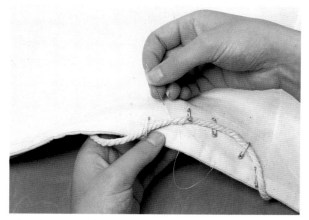

1 Drape the piping cord over the cushion cover, allowing it to fall naturally into curves and curlicues. Secure with safety pins. Allow the cord to travel across the reverse, as well as the face, of the cover for a flowing, naturalistic effect. Knot the loose ends together and tie each off in a simple knot.

2 Slip stitch the cord securely in place, using small stitches which pass through, rather than over, the entire surface of the cord. Remove the safety pins.

## ROSE APPLIQUÉ WITH RAFFIA TASSELS

1 To make a raffia tassel, first loop approximately 15 strands of raffia around your hand.

2 Place builder's brick line in a loop at the top end of the raffia, with the loop pointing downwards. Begin whipping the line around itself, starting at the looped end of the raffia (which will become the head of the tassel) and working down towards the skirt. ▶

69

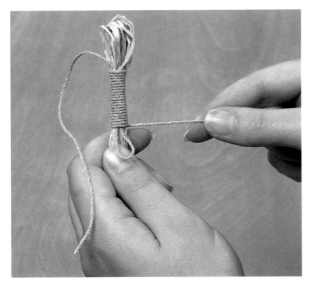

3 Continue wrapping the line evenly and tightly around the raffia until you reach the end of the loop of brick line.

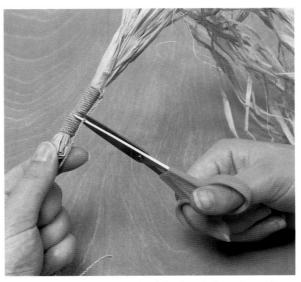

4 Pass the working end of the brick line through the loop. Cut the end so that it is approximately 2 cm/¾ in long.

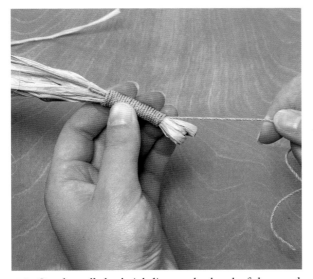

5 Gently pull the brick line at the head of the tassel to pull through the other, cut end, then work both ends securely into the neck binding. Make three more tassels in the same way.

6 Stitch the sisal rope in place around the border of the cushion cover. Slip stitch a tassel to each corner of the cover, and trim the ends of the raffia skirts to the desired length. Embellish the cover further by sewing on buttons, if desired.

# BEAUTIFUL BATIK

*Originating in Java, the technique of batik involves making designs on fabric by waxing parts not to be dyed. This cushion cover uses four different-coloured dyes to build up the rich pattern. The batik materials are widely available from specialist suppliers.*

YOU WILL NEED
80 cm/32 in of 90 cm-/36 in-wide white cotton fabric
washing soda
paper
black felt-tipped pen
250 g/9 oz batik wax
double boiler
adjustable tapestry frame
drawing pins
tjanting for applying the wax
kitchen towel
old paintbrush
bucket
urea
procion 'm' dyes in chrome yellow, turquoise,
peacock blue and navy
cooking salt
rubber gloves
sewing thread
press-and-close fastening or press fastener
30 cm-/12 in-square cushion pad

1 Wash the fabric thoroughly, and soak it in a solution of washing soda overnight to remove all traces of fabric finish. Rinse and allow to dry. Cut one 46 cm/18½ in square and two 46 x 30 cm/ 18½ x 12 in rectangles of fabric. Draw out the design from the back of the book on to a 40 cm/16 in square of paper and go over the lines with a felt-tipped pen. Trace the design on to the centre of the fabric with a pencil.

2 Heat the wax to between 50°C/122°F and 60°C/140°F in the double boiler. Stretch the fabric square on to the tapestry frame with pins. Using a tjanting, begin to wax the areas you want to remain white (the wax must penetrate the fabric so that it looks wet). Use a pad of kitchen towel to prevent drips.

3 For larger areas of the design, carefully outline them with the tjanting first and then fill them in using the old paintbrush.

4 Once all the white areas have been waxed, turn the frame over and, if necessary, rewax any areas where the wax has not penetrated completely. Leave to dry thoroughly. Next, prepare a yellow dye bath (see below). Add the batik square and the two rectangles to the bucket, and stir continuously for six minutes. Dissolve 15 ml/1 tbsp of soda in a little warm water and add this to the bucket. Leave the fabric to soak for a further 45 minutes, stirring occasionally. Remove the fabric and rinse it in cold water until the water runs clear, then hang it out to dry. Once dry, wax the areas that are to stay yellow.

5 Prepare a turquoise dye bath and immerse the fabric for 45 minutes. Once rinsed and dry, wax the areas that are to remain green. Prepare a peacock-blue dye bath using 10 ml/2 tsp of dye this time, and leave the fabric in the dye bath for up to an hour. Once the fabric is rinsed and dry, wax the areas that are to remain blue-green. Plunge the fabric into very cold water to "crack" some of the large areas of wax. Prepare a dye bath using 15 ml/1 tbsp of navy dye. Leave the fabric to soak for several hours, then rinse and leave to dry.

## PREPARING THE CHROME YELLOW DYE

Half fill a bucket with cold water. Dissolve 30 ml/2 tbsp of urea in 600 ml/1 pt of lukewarm water. In a separate container mix 5 ml/1 tsp of chrome yellow dye to a paste. Stir the urea solution into the dye paste and pour into the bucket. Dissolve 60 ml/4 tbsp of salt in 600 ml/1 pt of lukewarm water and add to the bucket.

TIP Wear rubber gloves throughout the dyeing process in order to prevent the wax and dye from harming your hands.

6 Protect your ironing board with an old sheet or cover. Place the batik between several layers of newspaper, and iron over it to melt the wax. Keep replacing the paper until most of the wax has been removed. The last traces of wax can be removed by dry cleaning or by immersing the fabric in boiling water. Press all the pieces while they are still damp.

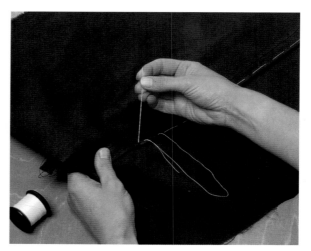

7 Stitch a small hem along the long edge of each rectangle of fabric. Overlap the hems to make a 46 cm/18½ in square with right sides facing up, then pin and tack together.

8 With right sides facing, pin the front and back of the cushion together. Stitch around the outside edge of the batik. Trim the seams, clip the corners and turn right side out. Remove the tacking.

9 Ease out the corners and press the seams. Pin and stitch close to the inside edge of the border, and trim the threads. Sew a small piece of press-and-close fastening or a press fastener to the opening edges of the cover. Insert the pad and close the fastening.

# IN THE ROUND

*A luxurious velvet bolster looks good on a window seat or adorning a chaise-longue. Use up left-over furnishing fabrics to make this simple patchwork cushion formed from strips. Trim the gathered ends with self-cover buttons, or add tassels to finish if you prefer.*

### YOU WILL NEED
45 cm-/18 in-long bolster cushion pad
pinking shears
remnants of velvet in orange, dark green, light green and lilac
sewing thread
vanishing fabric marker
two self-cover buttons
vanishing fabric marker

1 Measure the circumference of the bolster pad. Using pinking shears, cut one piece of orange velvet 21 cm/8¼ in wide, two pieces each of light green 7.5 cm/3 in wide, dark green 10 cm/4 in wide, and lilac 17 cm/6½ in wide by the measurement plus 3 cm/1¼ in. Pin and machine stitch the strips together by the longest edges as shown.

2 Fold the patched piece in half widthways, with right sides facing and the raw edges matching. Pin and machine stitch the seam to form a tube. Turn the cover right side out.

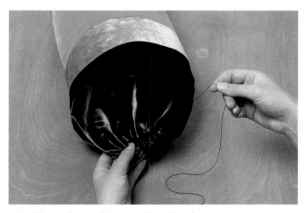

3 Place the cushion pad inside the cover. Using a double thread, run a gathering thread around each end. Draw up the thread, tuck the raw edges inside and stitch to secure.

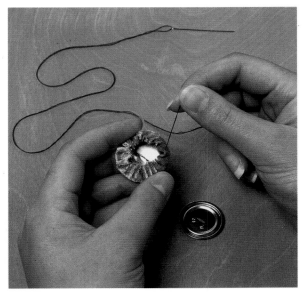

4 Using the vanishing fabric marker, draw around both of the self-cover buttons on the wrong side of a piece of light green velvet, adding a 6 mm/¼ in seam allowance. Cut out the circles.

5 Cover each button using a button maker, or simply sew a running stitch around the edge of each circle and pull up the thread to gather the fabric. Press the backs of the buttons into place.

6 Stitch a covered button over the gathered edge at each end of the bolster. ▶

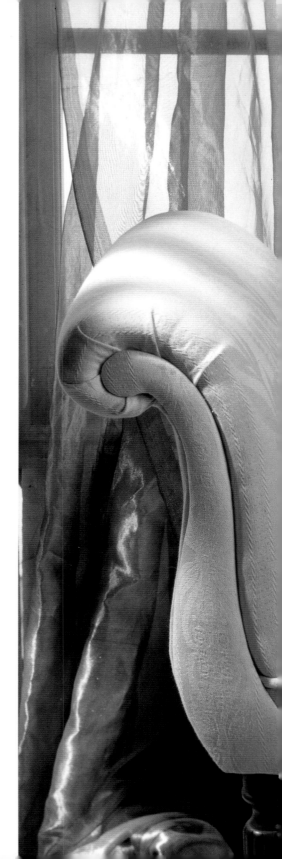

*Above: This simple bolster cushion was made from a single piece of velvet and trimmed with wide ribbon. The inner section is lined with toning fabric, and the ends simply gathered around the cushion pad and then wrapped with cord.*